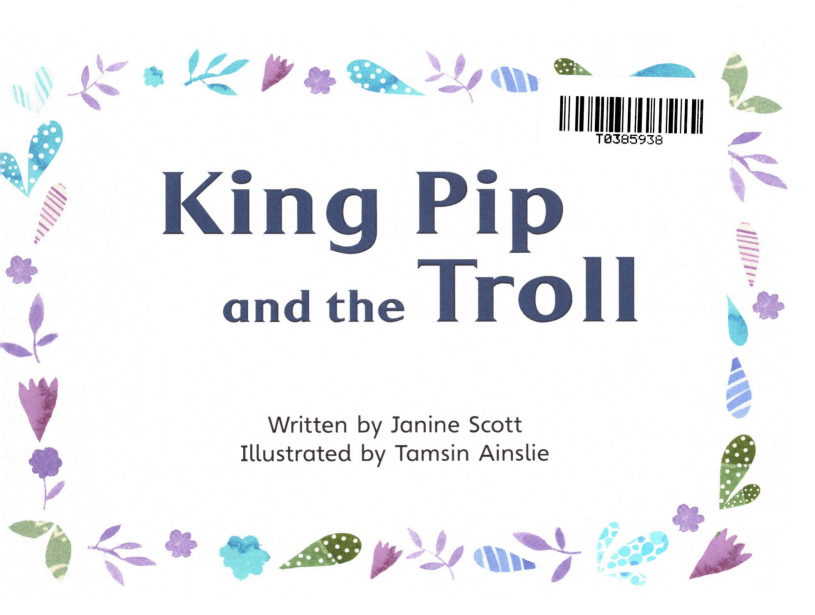

King Pip
and the Troll

Written by Janine Scott
Illustrated by Tamsin Ainslie

King Pip went to cross
the river.

A troll was on the bridge.

"Get off my bridge,"
said the troll.

He was in a mood.

3

A bear came to help.
"I have big claws," said the bear.

"I am not afraid of you,"
said the troll.

A crocodile came to help.
"I have big teeth," said the crocodile.

"I am not afraid of you,"
said the troll.

A goat came to help.
"I have big horns," said the goat.

8

"I am not afraid of you,"
said the troll.

"Let me help you," said a bug.
"I have lots of legs."

"Eek!" said the troll.
"I **am** afraid of ..."

"... bugs!"